G000140839

THE PURSUIT OF HAPPINESS AT WORK

*A Practical Guide to Having
a Purpose-Filled Career*

JAMES NIXON

Nixon Interests Publishing LLC

The Pursuit of Happiness at Work:
A Practical Guide to Having a Purpose-Filled Career

Published by Nixon Interests Publishing LLC

Nixon Interests Publishing LLC
E-mail: james@jamesnixonjr.com

Limit of Liability/Disclaimer of Warranty:

Publishing and editorial team:
Author Bridge Media, www.AuthorBridgeMedia.com
Project Manager and Editorial Director: Helen Chang
Publishing Manager: Laurie Aranda
Cover Designer: Mark Gelotte

Library of Congress Control Number: 2020923512
ISBN: 978-1-7361742-0-3 – softcover
978-1-7361742-1-0 – ebook

Ordering Information:
Quantity sales. Special discounts are available on quantity purchases by corporations, associations, and others. For details, contact the publisher at james@jamesnixonjr.com.

Printed in the United States of America

DEDICATION

The two most important days in your
life are the day you are born and
the day you find out why.

—Mark Twain

This book is dedicated to my parents, who made
the first day possible, and to the many teachers
throughout my life who helped me find out why.

CONTENTS

ACKNOWLEDGMENTS

The process of writing a book is challenging, to say the least—fraught with frustrations, blocks, and pitfalls. Never have I required an equal amount of mental stamina. However, I have also found this experience both humbling and gratifying, for this book enables me to fulfill my life's purpose of helping others to succeed—in this case in their careers. I thank God for blessing me with this amazing opportunity, and I thank the many extraordinary individuals who have played key roles both in helping me with this book and helping me become the man I am today.

First and foremost, thanks to my family, who have laid the foundation of who I am. In particular, Renee Clarke (grandmother), James Nixon Sr. (father), Renee Clarke Nixon (mother), and Nicole Nixon (sister). Thanks to my aunts, uncles, and cousins who have also played a key role in raising me, supporting me, and instilling in me the importance of education and service. In particular, Kent Nelson, Jean Nelson,

Chris Roberts, Joan Roberts, Mike Roberts, Jason Roberts, Kristen Roberts, Glenn Brue, Pam Brue, Beatrice Hofman, Lauren Thompson, Annie Nixon, Donnell Nixon, and Walter Benjamin.

To my amazing wife, Nicole, thank you for providing encouragement through this mentally exhausting exercise. You have stood by my side from day one and have supported me throughout this process. I love you.

Thanks to my in-laws for their love and support: Etienne Bertrand (father-in-law), Beryl Bertrand (mother-in-law), Jean-Philippe Bertrand (brother-in-law), L'Tanya Martin (aunt-in-law), and Andre Bertrand (uncle-in-law).

There is an African proverb that says, "It takes a village to raise a child," and I have been blessed to have a village of both family by blood and family by choice. I thank my mentors who have played my village's role of "elder" by teaching me and guiding me, and who continue to inspire me to reach for the stars: Reginald Van Lee, Michael Hyter, Mario Pipkin, George Corbin, Virgil Smith, Maryann Riggs, Tim McChristian, Jerry Levy, and Bob Logan. Thanks to my friends who have always supported me and told me the truth, whether I liked it or not. You keep me focused and grounded. A special thanks to the friends who helped me with this book: Kaplan Mobray, Steve Tozin, Ian Ramcheran, Jean Paul Richardson, James Reid, and Theodore Boykin.

Thanks to the organizations and their leaders who have given me the opportunity to work, learn, and grow as I pursued my own personal journey of happiness at work. I use the valuable lessons you have taught every day, and I have included them as foundational building blocks in this book.

To the people who give me the privilege and honor of being their mentor and coach—thank you. I am humbled by you and grateful that you give me the opportunity to fulfill my life's purpose. You are a major source of inspiration for this book.

Finally, deepest gratitude goes to Helen Chang, whose guidance, writing, and editing have made this book significantly better than it ever could have been without her.

Overview

The human spirit needs to accomplish,
to achieve, to triumph to be happy.

—Ben Stein

The Pursuit of Happiness at Work

Chris Gardner understood the power of finding
happiness through work. His story became the basis
of the blockbuster movie *The Pursuit of Happyness*,
starring actor Will Smith. Chris overcame incredible
challenges to achieve his dream job and life.
Following a business failure, Chris went through
utter devastation: abandonment by his wife, single
fatherhood of a young son, eviction, homelessness,
sleeping in public bathrooms, and doing job
interviews fresh from jail.

Despite the obstacles, Chris believed his talents could
bring both happiness and success to his family, so
he never gave up. He kept planning and pursuing his

dream job in the financial sector. Eventually, Chris achieved it, becoming a top wealth manager on Wall Street.

Chris always believed he could have happiness at work—and in his life. In his story, we're reminded that "the pursuit of happiness" is promised in the U.S. Declaration of Independence. As was true for Chris, it's your right to seek happiness—in your life and work.

But that's easy to forget.

Unhappiness at Work

Too often, work is something we have to "get through." Many of us dread Mondays, while thanking goodness for Fridays. We put up with toxic corporate cultures, avoid bosses we believe don't understand us, and disengage from companies we don't think care about us.

Maybe we started a job excited about making a difference. But over time, it turned into drudgery and even survival. Maybe it's a job that others hunger to get—offering prestige, a big office, and a high salary—yet we don't like the actual work we do. We have opportunities to grow, but not in the direction that truly fulfills us. We don't feel like we fit in. We know we should be grateful, but we're not.

In this context, it's easy to fall into the trap of believing that it's normal to go through every day feeling unfulfilled, feeling frustrated, wondering whether there's more—more in terms of being challenged, being inspired, having a purpose. More in terms of feeling that you've left your mark. That you've done things worth bragging about. Not necessarily more money—although that's welcome—but more in terms of happiness.

Where is our happiness? Most of us think of happiness as enjoying our personal lives while slogging through misery at work. We spend our days working without joy, just so we can experience happiness during our off-hours, weekends, and vacations.

But it doesn't have to be that way. You can find happiness in both your personal life and work. We were born to fulfill our life purpose—both in our work and personal lives. When we do, we contribute to others and experience joy in all aspects of our lives.

THE PURSUIT OF HAPPINESS AT WORK

Even in the worst of economic times, our lives are not just about finding work. Our lives are about pursuing our definition of happiness at work—in the jobs we already have, and the new jobs we might seek.

My Pursuit of Happiness at Work

My pursuit of happiness at work could be its own movie.

I've been the proverbial fish out of water, working for a paycheck. When I graduated from college, I started on a career track that I thought would fulfill all my ambitions. I was good at what I did, but I didn't align with it. It didn't make me happy.

My dissatisfaction propelled me to think deeply about what I really wanted—to work at a supportive place, with a capable leader, doing what I was gifted to do—so that I could experience happiness at work.

Since then, I've achieved happiness in my career, working for industry-leading companies—including Microsoft, CNN, the New York Times Company, Deloitte, Marriott, and Hilton—in jobs that truly brought out my skills and aligned with my purpose. I've coached other career professionals and spoken at organizations and conferences—empowering hundreds of others to either design their job so that it brings them immense joy, or to acknowledge they need a new position and then go out and get it.

I've developed these processes into an effective system that helps people pursue happiness and turn work into their ideal job. I call it the L.A.W. method—Learn, Assess, Walk.

The L.A.W. Method

Learn your definition of happiness at work.
Assess whether you are happy in your role.
Walk toward an opportunity that will make you happy.

Now, I'm sharing these proven strategies with you through this practical guidebook. Your perfect job is possible.

You Deserve Happiness

Everyone deserves a career that brings them happiness, and the possibility is waiting for us all. You may look around and see the success of others and think it's unattainable. But what shines isn't always gold. The people who typically appear as if they have it all together are usually the ones who don't.

The title, the money, the prestige? Those things don't necessarily translate into happiness at work, and they don't define you. What defines you is the impact you make, the way you feel, and how you're able to contribute to society. If you don't feel you're making an impact and blessing the world with everything that you have, then you're not living your purpose.

I'm guessing you don't want to be one of those people who resigns yourself to "the way things are." Take control of your career, find your purpose, and pursue your own happiness.

CHAPTER 1

The Career Happiness Guide

There is no passion to be found in playing small—
in settling for a life that is less than you are capable
of living.

—Nelson Mandela

Your Most Valuable Resource

The Pursuit of Happiness at Work is a global
phenomenon that is tracked and reported on annually
in the World Happiness Report, which ranks over
one hundred countries by how happy their citizens
perceive themselves to be.

In the United States, the pursuit of happiness is so
important that it was written into the Declaration
of Independence, the founding act of law that
established the US as a sovereign and independent
nation. The document states that all humans have the
unalienable rights of "Life, Liberty and the pursuit of

Happiness." And this happiness applies to all aspects of life, including work.

The average American lives seventy-nine years and spends approximately ninety thousand hours working—time taken away from the things that are truly important: family, friends, hobbies, and activities that make us really happy.

Research shows that 53 percent of Americans spend those work hours deeply unhappy. What's even more heartbreaking is that most of them submit to their situation and never try to improve it. They see it as inevitable.

They couldn't be more wrong.

Your work *can* be meaningful. You can be happy in your role—when you live your purpose and feel you're accomplishing something. But how do you get to a place where you feel that you're making a contribution? Where you're passionate, committed, and can make a real difference? The Declaration of Independence states that we all have the unalienable right to pursue happiness ... All you have to do is follow the L.A.W.—Learn, Assess, Walk—to achieve that happiness.

LEARN Your Definition of Happiness at Work. The first step is to learn about your own needs and desires. What are your natural talents? What makes a job a good fit? When you know your purpose and your strengths, you can start to apply them.

ASSESS Whether You Are Happy in Your Role. Next, you need to assess your current work situation. Are you happy? Your company wants you to love your job as much as you want that happiness. Working together, you can achieve incredible things.

WALK Toward an Opportunity That Will Make You Happy. Sometimes, it just isn't the right fit, and it's time to walk away and set off on a new journey. I'll take you through the tricks for finding, applying to, and getting the perfect job.

This is a practical methodology that I've honed over decades in the workplace. It's landed me amazing jobs and has helped countless others to rediscover happiness at work.

A Journey of Self Discovery

Truth is, I haven't always found happiness at work. Early in my career, I landed a great management consulting job. After working there for some time, I was surprised to find that I wasn't happy. Yes, I was making good money. Yes, I was at a prestigious firm. Yes, I was helping clients solve big problems. I was good at it too.

But I wasn't happy.

Because every project was different, I couldn't build a foundation. I couldn't specialize. That environment may work for others, but my passion was digging deep into a subject, so my aspirations didn't fit the needs of the job. And because projects were assigned from above, I couldn't pick the work I was interested in. I had a background in technology and telecommunications, and most of the work I was given fit that very narrow scope. But I wanted to do more. I wanted to learn, expand, and experience new things.

Here I was at a job with great pay and plentiful opportunities, but it just didn't feel right. I wasn't passionate. I wasn't giving it my all. Every day I went to work, I felt lost. I didn't volunteer for new projects.

I didn't get excited about work coming down the pipeline. I was going through the motions.

I knew something had to change.

I had to figure out what I really wanted. I needed to examine my wants and desires. What would make me happy? What kind of career did I want? What was I good at? And how could I go and get it?

That low point in my career put me on a journey. It helped me realize nothing else matters from a work perspective if you're not happy. It compelled me to find out how to become happy. I didn't have all the answers yet. But I knew there was a path forward, and that it was one I was determined to walk.

Since then, I've honed my process for understanding what drives me, finding ways to apply my passions at my current position, and knowing how to move on when I need to—all to achieve not just a job, but also happiness at work. In the chapters to come, I'll show you how to apply this process to your own career.

This is your opportunity to pursue happiness, and to make every job the ideal one.

The Guide

This practical guide will show you the steps to an exciting and purposeful career that will bring you happiness. I'll help you achieve your vision by outlining a straightforward approach with step-by-step instructions for taking control of your career. No matter your personality type, your gifts or abilities, or whether you're an extrovert or introvert, these detailed examples, references, and tools will guide you throughout the process.

We'll learn what kind of job makes you most happy, how to turn your current role into one that satisfies those goals, and what's next as you set off on this journey of discovery.

Using the L.A.W. method, this playbook covers these topics:

Learn

Chapter 2: Choose a New Meaning of Success—happiness and financial stability

Chapter 3: Create Happiness at Work—three rules of work happiness

Assess

Chapter 4: Grow as a Leader—a proven formula for career success

Chapter 5: Determine Your Unique Strengths—ways to leverage your strengths

Chapter 6: Discover Opportunities—strategies to find the best fit

Walk

Chapter 7: Plan Your Ideal Job—a proven method for planning success

Chapter 8: Execute the Search—keys to landing the right job

Chapter 9: Mission Accomplished—ways to successfully transition to your new role

As you follow this guide, I suggest taking it chapter by chapter. Each step builds on the next. Each piece you understand about yourself takes you closer to creating your ideal job. You'll gain access to proven resources, processes, strategies, and checklists for what to do each step of the way.

You'll also hear stories from my own and others' career paths. Although I have changed some names and details to honor confidentiality, all the stories are true. Most importantly, in following these strategies, you'll have confidence in moving toward your best position. You'll know how to land not just any job, but a job that brings you greatest happiness.

The first step on this journey is asking yourself what career success looks like for you.

L	**Choose a New Meaning**
E	**of Success**
A	The only way to do great work is to love
R	what you do.
N	—Steve Jobs

Money versus Happiness

People have asked me, "What's more important at work? To make money, or to be happy?"

As children, we think that happiness is more important than money. But as adults, we think money is more important. I now know it's possible to have both.

Over 80 percent of participants in a research study indicated that money can't buy happiness. Rather, the participants expressed that happiness came from gaining a sense of purpose by making an impact. They also said they were happy when working in a caring and supportive environment where they could learn, grow, be authentic, and create meaningful social bonds with colleagues, co-workers, and customers. Finally, happiness resulted from being challenged. Moreover, people enjoyed celebrating their wins and learning from their mistakes.

When people are able to achieve happiness at work, they're more likely to have success, and with success comes money. Think of money not as a goal, then, but as a natural outcome of the goal of happiness.

"Good Enough" Money

As Americans, we're sold a dream that getting rich means we'll be happy.

In one poll published by Seniorliving.org, Americans said the definition of rich is having an annual salary of at least $300,000 and a net worth of at least $2.3 million dollars. That's nice, but most of us don't earn that much and may never reach that net worth.

That's why achieving happiness isn't about trying to get rich, but rather about financial stability. In other words, "good enough" money.

"Good enough" money means that you can consistently meet the needs of your household—not just the necessities like food, shelter, and educational needs for your children, but also essential perks like yearly holidays. With financial stability you can meet those needs comfortably while maintaining an emergency fund (three to six months of living expenses) and saving for retirement.

Unfortunately, I learned the hard way how important financial stability is to happiness at work. When I was a little over a decade into my career, my mother was diagnosed with cancer. She had to undergo a number of costly treatments, and I wanted to help support her. But I couldn't afford the medical expense. Here I was, facing a serious illness in my family, but due to my enormous financial debt, I didn't have the resources to help. I was devastated—not only by my mother's illness, but also by my financial situation. At that time I was single, in great health, and spent much of my limited resources "living life." I always figured that I would build financial stability when I was older.

My mother's illness caught me off guard. I wasn't prepared, and I didn't handle it well. It also had a negative impact on my work as I worried constantly, became distant from my team, and was unable to focus on my projects.

I did my best to support my mother emotionally, and being the fighter that she is, she eventually overcame the cancer. After that, I swore I would make sure to prepare myself and always be financially stable. For me, financial stability is a key anchor not only for career success, but also success in life.

I have found that combining happiness at work with financial stability provides the foundation to achieve real and lasting success.

But you have to define happiness for yourself. And you have to ask what success really means to you. Does happiness at work and financial stability create lasting success for you?

> Visit my website for tips on achieving financial stability: ThePursuitOfHappinessAtWork.com.

CHAPTER 3

L
E
A   **Create Happiness**
R   **at Work**
N

Trust the quality of what you know,
not the quantity.

—Mr. Miyagi, The Karate Kid

Wax On, Wax Off

You may be familiar with one of my favorite movies,
The Karate Kid, but I bet you've never considered
it as a master-class metaphor for the three rules of
happiness at work. The story is about a young man,
Daniel, dealing with bullies at school. He wants to
defend himself so he signs up for karate lessons, only
to learn that the bullies attend and teach in the dojo.
He meets Mr. Miyagi, the building manager of the
apartment where he lives, who agrees to teach him
how to fight.

But when the lessons begin, Daniel is shocked that they're nothing like what the boys in the dojo are learning. Instead, Mr. Miyagi assigns manual tasks: Daniel has to use sandpaper to smooth down the floor in a certain way, paint the house a certain way, and of course, wax the car. Wax on, wax off, breathe in, breathe out. According to Daniel's internal perspective, he's just doing manual labor.

Fortunately, Daniel voices his perspective to Mr. Miyagi before quitting (unlike what most people do in similar situations). Mr. Miyagi shows Daniel everything he has learned without even knowing it: blocking, punching, and mastering internal calm. With this new perspective, Daniel takes to his training like a fish to water. Spoiler alert: He goes on to beat his bullies and win the All Valley Karate Tournament.

Daniel's story sharply illustrates the three rules for creating happiness at work. Rule No. 1: Find a job that plays to your strengths. Rule No. 2: Nurture a caring work environment. Rule No. 3: Manage your perspective.

No matter what stage you're at in your career, you can enhance your work life with these three rules. This is part of the L of the L.A.W. method—Learn Your

Definition of Happiness at Work. By following these rules, you lay the framework for achieving your purpose and finding lasting happiness from your career.

Rule No. 1: Play to Your Strengths.

Gallup's research suggests that employees who leverage their unique strengths at work are much happier. This is because when we're able to play to our strengths, we can accomplish more. And when we feel good about what we're doing, whether that's working toward something or making a difference in the organization, we feel more job satisfaction. In essence, it feels good to be good at what you do. That's why playing to your strengths is so important.

However, some of us don't know what we're good at. This is why determining your strengths is so important. We'll go into that in more detail in chapter 5.

Rule No. 2: Nurture a Caring Work Environment.

Every person needs a caring and nurturing support system, one that helps them grow and achieve greatness. There are many factors that contribute to a positive work environment, including a productive atmosphere and core-values alignment.

I love work environments that are so quiet you can hear a pin drop. My wife, however, likes to work with a TV or music in the background. A productive atmosphere will be different for every person, and it's essential to find your fit. What helps you stay focused? You want to be in balance so that you can accomplish all the things that are coming your way.

Seek out open dialogue with team members about how you each work best and how you can align with each other. You could create quiet zones or no-meeting Fridays—whatever works best for the group members.

In addition, how you see the world must absolutely overlap with how your current company (or the one you wish to work for) sees the world. The more these things are aligned, the happier you will be. Remember, these are your values. This is what you believe. And if your company and you have different or opposing beliefs, you'll be stuck going against your values for the sake of a paycheck. This is something you need to know when you start a new job, because it's impossible to change after the fact.

Compassionate team members

A common misconception about work is that it's a zero-sum game. The truth is, you don't have to lose for someone else to win, and you want to be in an environment with people who want to help you win. When seeking to create a caring environment, focus on being positive, authentic, respectful, and empathetic. You can foster a positive workspace by being the place where change starts.

If your workplace isn't living up to what it could be, think about what can be done to fix it. Have some honest conversations with your team about how they want to interact. Get your boss involved, and make sure you're aligned and on the same page. Team culture is something you build, not something that just happens by chance.

A Great Boss

Speaking of your boss: People don't leave jobs. They leave managers. To be at your best, you want a leader who communicates a clear vision; sets and manages expectations; fosters an environment for learning, sharing, and taking risks; rewards good performance; and possesses a great leadership style. One of the things that I find helpful when trying to determine how well a potential boss and I will relate is to understand his or her leadership style. My leadership style, for example, is Transformational Leadership.

Transformational leaders value employees and help them unlock their potential to innovate and create change that will grow and shape the future success of the company. If my potential boss is also a transformational leader or possesses attributes of transformational leadership, then we are typically a match made in heaven.

> Visit my website for more information:
> ThePursuitOfHappinessAtWork.com.

Sometimes, however, your style just doesn't gel with your boss's. So, before you leave a position, talk with your manager about your differing leadership styles and how they could best work together. You'd be surprised at how effective an open and honest dialog can be.

Rule No. 3: Manage Your Perspective.

You could have the greatest job in the world. You could work in the most caring and nurturing workplace. But if you don't acknowledge this and appreciate the situation, you'll never be happy.

Not every day at work is going to be sunny. It's up to us to do our part to acknowledge the silver lining and to appreciate when the sunny days return. That's easier said than done, of course. So how do you manage your perspective? By understanding the internal factors and the external factors.

In any situation, you need to understand what success looks like for you, whether in regard to a specific project, a team member, or progressing toward your larger career goals. You also need to understand yourself and what drives you. That requires a high EQ, or emotional intelligence, as explained in Daniel Goleman's book *Emotional Intelligence*. Understanding yourself and your definition of success will help you relieve stress and practice self-control, which are keys to managing any situation.

Externally, sometimes you have to realize that it's not all about you. People have complicated lives, and sometimes you only see the tip of the iceberg. Try to understand the things that are happening around you from the perspective of others. Walk in their shoes. What are they feeling? How is this affecting them? You might be surprised to learn how much more complicated an issue is than the small piece you're dealing with personally.

There's a great saying: "There are three sides to every story: your version, the other person's version, and the truth." When you understand how you feel about something, and you understand how the other person feels, you get as close as possible to the truth. And once you have the truth, you have a clear context and can react appropriately.

A Formula for Happiness

Now that you can define what happiness at work means to you and how to create that happiness, it's time to talk about implementation. You need a framework that helps you apply your strengths and provides a straightforward way to measure whether you're hitting your goals. For that, I use a strategic model that accelerates career paths.

CHAPTER 4

A
S
S
E
S
S

Grow as a Leader

If you're quiet, you will not be discovered.

—Kaplan Mobray

Leadership is a Noun

One of the most influential people in my career was a man who had an upside-down chart on his wall.

Vince, a leader in the talent management space, took me on as his mentee and shared key experiences I would need to become a leader. The first time I stepped into his office, I noticed how everything had its place. The shelves showcased valuable collectibles from around the world. Photos on the walls showed him with dignitaries and loved ones.

On one wall, the company organization chart with more than one thousand positions hung upside down. When I asked about it, he grinned.

"My job is to empower everyone else by lifting them up and helping them to achieve greatness," he said. "That's why I'm at the bottom."

He was a transformational leader, and I vowed to become one too.

As we discussed my leadership development and career path, he advised me to consider four elements that can define a noun: ideas, products, places, and people.

In my jobs to date, I had created ideas as a management consultant and products as a technology expert. But he advised me to pursue places, either through assignments in different areas of the company or through international management experience, and people, through leadership.

Vince said, "Spending time overseas helps you develop your career by expanding your network and seeing the global marketplace from another perspective. It also gives you the opportunity to live an enriched life that comes from experiencing a different culture.

"You've created amazing ideas and awesome products, but those are things that you've done yourself," he said. "The true leader is one who is able to inspire others to create amazing ideas and products, to accomplish things that they didn't even think they could."

That made me think about what my purpose was. I wanted to be the kind of leader who inspired others to achieve greatness. This drive became a set of simple, repeatable processes that I shared with others.

The next component in the L.A.W. method for pursuit of happiness at work is the A step, where we Assess Whether You Are Happy in Your Role.

The P.I.E. Model

I'm very keen on identifying simple, straightforward, and repeatable processes that work. That's why I knew how important it was to find a formula that would help define the path to career success.

To do that, I attended leadership training courses. I took dozens of leadership assessments. I read numerous books and articles and watched tons of lectures on leadership. And I discovered the following formula that has repeatedly developed strong leaders.

For forty years, Harvey J. Coleman, the founder of Coleman Management Consultants, studied leaders at Fortune 100 companies, governmental agencies, and nonprofit organizations. In his book *Empowering Yourself*, he shares how professionals move from good technicians to industry leaders.

It's called the P.I.E. model. P.I.E. stands for Performance, Image, and Exposure.

Performance: Performance is doing A+ quality work. It means not just delivering, but exceeding what you've been hired to do. Most people believe P makes up a huge part of the success pie. But according to Coleman, it contributes just 10 percent. That's because you were hired to perform. Everyone expects their employees to excel, and even delivering above and beyond what's expected is still just delivering.

Image: An image is your personal brand. It's the way you walk. The way you sit. The clothes you wear. How you say things. How you treat others. Your personal brand is extremely important. It takes a long time to build, and you can lose it in a heartbeat by damaging your credibility. To build and maintain your personal brand, you need to protect it.

One extraordinary expert on personal branding is Kaplan Mobray, author of *The 10Ks of Personal Branding*. Kaplan provides easy-to-follow instructions and valuable tips to develop and maintain an excellent personal brand. I've found them essential to ensuring my success.

While performance is only 10 percent of your career success pie, your personal brand makes up 30 percent. Think about how much better it feels to work in a caring environment, with people who are compassionate and great team players. That's how you want people to think about you. Are you a team player? Are you compassionate? Are you the go-to person? Are you the one they want to be associated with? Develop your image carefully, and guard it with your life.

Exposure: Who knows you, and what do they know about you? Exposure is the portion of the P.I.E. model that brings us face-to-face with the people game. Your success has a lot to do with you, but it has equally, if not more, to do with the others around you. You can't promote yourself. Trust me—I've tried. And to get someone to want to boost your career, you need people to speak well of you and tout your successes and strengths. Then someone who has the power to help you will want to see you do well. That's why exposure is the full remaining 60 percent of the P.I.E. model.

Exposure is closely tied to the first two rules. If you can't perform, and don't have a good brand, you'll have exposure all right. But it will be negative. You have to make sure that the first two are in place so that when you get exposure, people are receptive to it. You have to come across as credible and authentic.

You get exposure if you do well and your work is passed up the chain of command. You also receive exposure by volunteering for affinity groups or community service organizations. Consider whether leaders in your organization are part of specific groups, and join those. Just be sure to be authentic, rather than appearing to be just playing along to get some alone time with the boss.

Another great way to get exposure is to go outside your job altogether. You can become a thought leader, giving lectures or writing a book. Author Bridge Media is an example of a company that supports thought leaders in writing their own books. You could also write articles on LinkedIn. Your goal is to get your voice out there in a credible, authentic way.

For some people, exposure is easy. But not everyone is an extrovert. And that can make exposure feel daunting. What introvert wants to hobnob at happy hour, give speeches, and master small talk? But you don't have to be an extrovert to get exposure. I know. I'm not!

Be a thought leader by writing articles. Do good work that gets passed up the chain. And when you do get exposure, manage it in ways that work for you. For instance, I find that taking breaks during networking events helps me recharge so I have the energy to make a lasting impression on others.

How to Have No Effort

P.I.E. was the formula that I had been searching for: simple, straightforward, and repeatable. I was in heaven.

Now that I knew this definition of success—
performance + image + exposure = 100 percent—
I knew this was how I would be successful. Given
my pragmatic nature, I wanted to align my efforts
with the formula. I had to make sure that I spent
30 percent of my effort developing a great personal
brand. And with exposure accounting for 60 percent,
it was clear that I should focus most of my efforts
there.

In the P.I.E. model, only 10 percent of success is based
on performance. As I learned this model, I wondered
how I could provide excellent performance while
using the lowest percentage of effort. I knew it was
possible, because I'd seen it done before.

CHAPTER 5

A
S
S
E
S
S

Determine Your Unique Strengths

We focus on what people's natural strengths are and spend our management time trying to find ways for them to use those strengths every day.

—Sheryl Sandberg

Break the Curve

When I was in business school, I had a friend who prepared for exams by socializing in bars. Mike never took notes, rarely asked questions, and never studied.

Yet after every test and exam, he broke the grade curve. Meanwhile, I studied for days just to match the curve. It was infuriating!

Because Mike spent so little time studying, he spent the balance of his time focusing on what I now understand as building his personal brand. He was a great communicator, the person everyone went to for advice, and a volunteer at community organizations. He also led the student venture-capital fund—all of which enhanced his brand.

I couldn't understand how Mike could put in so little effort and still achieve A+ grades. Finally, after weeks of pestering, he admitted he had a photographic memory. One of his unique attributes was that Mike could remember everything, down to the smallest detail. He could remember a number down to the third decimal point, etched perfectly in his memory. This gift allowed him to remember lessons and perform on exams almost effortlessly.

More critical was Mike's understanding of his unique skill. When you know your unique gifts, you can perform effortlessly too. The better you know your strengths, the more likely you'll be to align yourself in a role that will leverage your natural abilities and line up with your purpose. This is the next step in the A portion of the L.A.W. method, when you Assess Whether You Are Happy in Your Role. In looking at your current job or another position, you will focus on which roles showcase your unique strengths and enhance your brand, leadership, and happiness.

A Personal Skills Assessment

In my search for ways to achieve effortless peak performance, I learned about the Highlands Ability Battery.

The Highlands Ability Battery is a human assessment tool that objectively measures your natural abilities. Instead of being based on self-perception or opinion, it uses a series of brainteasers to measure abilities based on time or performance.

Many tests classify you by a certain number of simple characteristics, based on your answers to personality-based questions. The Highlands Ability Battery has a different level of fidelity, and I highly recommend taking it. It gives you a real understanding of your unique strengths and weaknesses, the kinds of jobs best aligned with those abilities, and the type of work environment you would thrive in. And that's just the beginning.

The Path to Success

Throughout my undergraduate and early career years, people would often tell me I was going to go far in life, and I could become a CEO and run a company one day. At first, I didn't believe them. I would think to myself, "Yeah, sure, you probably tell everyone that." But after hearing this feedback over and over again, I started to believe that I could become a CEO. If it was going to be, then it was up to me.

I decided that if I was going to become a CEO, I would need to follow the career path of a successful CEO. At the time, I most resonated with Kenneth Chenault, the former CEO of American Express, because he looked like me and made it big in corporate America. I started to follow Chenault's career path, trying to match mine to his. Almost everything he had done, I had done. This was my checklist:

Kenneth Chenault's Career Path	My Career Path
Chenault graduated from great universities with both undergraduate and graduate degrees.	I graduated from great universities with undergraduate and graduate degrees.
Chenault worked at a top management consulting firm.	I worked at a top management consulting firm.
Chenault joined a strategic planning group of an industry-leading company.	I joined a strategic planning group of an industry-leading company.
Chenault worked his way up, becoming CEO of American Express.	I planned to work my way up to become CEO of a large corporation.

But once I took the Highlands Ability Battery test, my perspective completely changed.

The Highlands Ability Battery explores the concept of a generalist versus a specialist. Generalists are people who have a variety of experiences and expertise. They have well-rounded knowledge and are able to connect dots where others don't see a link. Generalists' thoughts and perspectives are typically similar to those of others around them.

Specialists, on the other hand, like to master a body of knowledge or work and to develop a skill of their own. They have in-depth knowledge in that specific subject matter, which lets them make sense of new developments and opportunities. Specialists have a unique, individual way of looking at the world, which causes them to approach situations differently. I'm a specialist through and through, and I found this out during the assessment.

Think Dog

If I show you an image of a kitchen table, what do you associate that with? Most people say food, chair, family, or maybe even gathering.

When I saw this image during the assessment, I said dog. It went back to when I was a kid. Every time I ate at the kitchen table, our family dog begged for food. He nipped at my heels and whimpered. I was so annoyed! As an adult, every time I see a kitchen table, I think of that spoiled dog.

We each have our unique ways of seeing any given situation. These play to our strengths as generalists or specialists in global organizations. One of the turning points in my life was the realization that my unique way of interpreting situations didn't naturally align with my goal to be CEO of a large global organization.

One of the CEO's jobs is to be the public face of the company, not only for external resources but also for employees. That means leading employees and inspiring them to execute. In order to inspire employees, a CEO needs to be able to empathize with them. Empathy means seeing the world through other people's eyes, in order to feel what they feel and experience things as they do. This ability comes more naturally to a generalist, given that they're more likely to share many of the same thoughts and perspectives as others.

Specialists, on the other hand, have a unique, individual way of looking at the world, which causes them to approach situations differently. As a specialist, I wanted to "think dog" in my daily work. I knew I had the ability to come up with big ideas that others might not have, and that following my passion meant giving rein to those ideas.

With this new knowledge in hand, I altered my career path. Instead of following Chenault's footsteps, I aligned my path with a trajectory that would take advantage of my "dog strengths." I sought out opportunities that took advantage of my specialized mind-set—often these were positions where I could bring new technology and platforms into existing businesses, or help businesses think in new and exciting ways. By aligning my career path with my strengths, I found real happiness in my career.

To be clear, this by no means indicates that a specialist can *never* be a successful senior executive leader. But it does mean that achieving that level of success will take more effort than it will for someone whose thoughts and perspectives are similar to others around them. This additional effort could cause a specialist to spend more than 10 percent of their time on the P from P.I.E. However, it's up to each specialist to determine how being out of alignment with P.I.E. will impact their overall career. They may not mind putting in the extra work.

Know Your Strengths

Even after you take a skills assessment test, it's important to keep focused on how your strengths and weaknesses manifest in your career. That takes a lot of introspection. You intuitively know your strengths overall, but it's much harder to understand them thoroughly and to know how they might manifest in different situations.

I made a conscious decision to navigate my career based on my gift for specialization. And even though I continue to move up, I do so in a specialized way. If I'm offered an opportunity that I know won't suit my skills, I turn it down so I can continue to look for something that will make me happy. And that happiness has led me to be very successful, because it's infectious. It rubs off on others. People want to be around me, and living up to that inspires me to be more reliable and more valuable. It gives me more money and gets me promoted. My greatest happiness, however, comes from my understanding of who I am, which allows me to be true to myself and fulfill my purpose.

CHAPTER 6

A
S
S
E
S
S

Discover Opportunities

Decide what you want, and then act as if it were
impossible to fail.

—Brian Tracy

Discover Opportunities That Are Right for You

One young man I mentored had two opportunities he
could pursue. But he wasn't sure which would be a
better fit—which would make him happiest.

He needed to understand the opportunities before
him, and how his skills aligned with each position.
After taking the Highlands Ability Battery test, the
young man was amazed to see his abilities laid out
before him.

He quickly realized why his current role did not fit
him. The job called for quantitative data analysis, but

his strength was in creating relationships. With the test results, he also realized that the two new jobs he was considering were not right either. Instead, he needed to move toward business development, where he could apply his skills to sales targets and figures, while also working with people and helping them solve problems and form relationships.

Once he moved in that direction, it catapulted his career.

You've already done the work to identify your own strengths and unique talents. Now you need to identify roles and opportunities that align with these talents, because following your purpose is the path to true happiness. This is the last step in the A stage of the L.A.W. method, where you Assess Whether You Are Happy in Your Role. You may be surprised at how many opportunities there are at your current company to craft a job that fits your talents better. So let's talk about some tools, tips, and techniques for you to accomplish this goal.

Your Ideal Role

The first step to discovering your best opportunity is to draft your ideal job description. Start by digesting the results of your assessment. Critically examine what it said about you and how it makes you feel. Then start using those insights to draft your ideal job description. Ask yourself questions about that perfect job.

- What role would be a good fit for my skills?

- How much money is enough for me to be financially stable?

- What benefits do I desire?

- How much vacation time do I want?

- Where would my ideal role be located?

- Do I want to travel? If so, how much: 10 percent, 50 percent, 90 percent?

Now, I want you to go deeper. Ask questions based on specific things that you learned from your assessment.

- Should I be a people leader or an individual contributor?

- Should I work in a more creative role or an analytical role?

- Do I want a role where I juggle multiple things simultaneously? Or do I want a job where I can focus on a single task at any given time?

- Am I motivated by seeing tangible results? Or would I prefer to work in a more theoretical capacity?

That should give you a firm understanding of the kind of role you want. Next, examine *where* you want to work. What will the company be like?

- What type of company culture would I thrive in?

- Is diversity in the workplace important to me?

- What leadership style would I like my boss to have?

- Do I prefer working more with introverts or extroverts?

- Do I want to work in a job where I sit at my desk all day, or one where I'm required to move around?

- Do I prefer to work in an open environment, or have an office door to close?

- Is working virtually an important option for me?

The answers to many of these questions will connect to clear career recommendations that you can reference in your readout from the Highlands Ability Battery. For instance, when I was coming out of business school, I had two opportunities for work: an investment bank or consulting. The thought of sitting in front of a screen all day, looking at curves on a monitor and not being mobile, was an instant turnoff. I knew, based on my personality, that I wouldn't be happy there. I chose the consulting job.

Find the Gap

Once you've created your ideal job description, share it with a few mentors or colleagues you trust and get their take on it. Do they agree with what you've highlighted as your needs? Have they noticed anything about the way you work that the skills assessment missed?

Make tweaks based on their feedback, and then compare your ideal job to your current role. How well does it match your current job? Be honest with yourself. If the match is high, it's possible that the challenges you're experiencing with your job aren't due to the role itself, but rather how well you're managing your perspective. Are there other things that you can do to address that?

If your match is low, what is it about your job that's misaligned? Can those things be changed? Sit down with your boss and discuss your strengths and passions. Your boss wants you to be at your very best as much as you do! It's in his or her best interest to help you better tailor your job to that ideal description, or even to look for other internal opportunities that are better suited to your skills.

If they can't, then it is time to start looking for new roles that will better align with your ideal job description.

An External Search

Cast a wide net, focusing on responsibilities rather than role titles, and collect a large sample of role possibilities. Include any roles recommended by the assessment tools you've used. Review jobsites, explore different roles at companies that you're interested in, and note the things they're asking for. Keep in mind that the responsibilities of a position with the same title can differ from company to company.

Try to understand which roles best align with your unique makeup. Include any jobs that you find interesting, or that have a close fit to your unique abilities, even if they're in a very different industry than you're used to.

I have a group of mentors that I like to call my "Board of Directors." I go to them for advice and counsel repeatedly, and I also serve on other people's boards. I make sure to have a diverse set of mentors to ensure that I am getting advice from multiple vantage points.

Having this kind of consistent relationship means that they grow to know you well over time. When you reach this stage in your journey, take your list to your own board of directors. Hear their findings, and get advice about any roles you might not have thought to look into.

Narrow the Field

It's time to narrow it down to your top three. Pick three opportunities that match every one of your "must haves." Once you've selected your top three, try to find people who are in those roles in the industry you want to be in. And then, validate your hypotheses about the role by getting in touch and asking whether they'd mind talking to you a little about what their job entails.

When you meet the person, don't be afraid to talk about yourself. Explain your makeup, your strengths and interests, and why you think the role would be a good fit for you. Then ask them whether they agree. "In your experience as a director of marketing, does that make sense to you? What things am I missing?" Without having done the job, it's next to impossible to know every detail of what it requires, so these face-to-face meetings are beyond valuable.

Collect the information you need, and go back to your list. If there's something that aligns 80 percent with your ideal job, it's time to develop a plan for making your move.

CHAPTER 7

W
A
L
K

Plan Your Ideal Job

A goal without a plan is just a wish.

—Antoine de Saint-Exupéry

A Wish Is Better with a Plan

As I grew in my career, I looked for opportunities to check off the corporate experiences that my mentor Vince, who said "Leadership is a Noun", had suggested.

My next growth step was "places"—international management experience. I went to my network and started looking for positions that involved travel. I connected with a colleague in my network who worked for Marriott. The global hotel chain had opened a position to grow its digital platform worldwide. With his referral, I got the interview and a job offer.

At the same time, I received three other job offers, one from a news organization and two from tech companies. Suddenly, I had a difficult choice to make. Which of these opportunities best fit my goals? Where would I be happiest?

So I created a "perfect" job description. I asked myself what my goal was. Where did I really want to work? I wanted to travel. I wanted a boss I could learn from, a subject matter expert. And I wanted to make an impact.

Then I looked at all the job opportunities I had and overlapped them with my personal job description. One job stood out, hitting everything on my list of ideals: The international component was strong. My boss would be a Harvard MBA who had once owned his own consulting firm. It was a small team, but one that I could grow and make a difference.

I accepted the job with Marriott, and I found that I was right: it was the perfect fit.

Make a Plan

Your next step is to construct a career plan that will outline how you get from where you are today to where you want to be. By now, we are at the last stage of the L.A.W. method, the W of Walk Toward an Opportunity That Will Make You Happy.

When I coach mentees, I guide them to create a plan before searching for a job. The plan consists of several components.

Form a goal

You've already identified your ideal role. Now you need to break that job description down into your must-haves and your nice-to-haves.

Must-Haves	Nice-to-Haves
1. Have a social media marketing role.	1. Work in the tech industry.
2. Work in a midsize B2C company.	2. Have a good benefits package.
3. Earn at least $100,000 dollars annually.	3. Get three weeks' annual vacation.
4. Work remotely or be locally based, within a one-hour commute of your house.	

You should construct a S.M.A.R.T. goal that's based only on your must-haves: to obtain a locally based social media marketing role at a midsize business-to-consumer company, earning at least $100,000 annually, within one year.

Perform a skills gap assessment

The first step toward achieving your smart goal is to perform an analysis of your current skill set versus the skills you'll need for the job you want. Your gap analysis should take into account transferable skills. For instance, if you're a public relations specialist and want a role in social media marketing, your writing skills would be a transferable skill set.

Once you've determined how big the gap is in your skill set, make a plan for filling that gap. Read articles, take training courses, find someone to job shadow, and look for short-term jobs, paid or volunteer.

Leverage your network

Getting hired into a new role requires help from a village of supporters. Your network will play a key role in your job pursuit, including motivating you to keep going. They'll also help you get interviews. Roughly 48 percent of hires come from an employee referral, so you must tap your network to increase your likelihood of getting that dream job. Make sure your network includes coaches, mentors, co-workers, and friends. You can also connect with people at headhunting or job placement agencies.

Create or update your personal branding materials

We talked about how a strong personal brand is vital for achieving success in your current role. It's also critical for obtaining a new role. When searching for a new job, there are three essential tools for representing your personal brand:

- **Resume**. Your resume should highlight key skills and experiences that are transferable to your potential role. Consider having your resume developed by a professional resume writer. They'll know the latest techniques for positioning you as a qualified candidate, getting noticed by search engines, and helping you get the interview.

- **Cover letter**. Use this document to explain why your skills and experiences are a good fit for the job. Call out transferable skills and identify strengths that the interviewer may not see from your resume alone. Tailor your cover letter to each specific job that you apply for.

- **LinkedIn**. Boost your credibility and visibility with a strong LinkedIn profile. Have a professional headshot, ensure your page has no typos or grammatical errors, and fill in any missing sections in your skills and work history.

> Visit my website for helpful tips on resumes, cover letters, and LinkedIn: ThePursuitOfHappinessAtWork.com.

Paint a picture of your financial future

A crucial factor to consider when switching careers is the impact on your finances. Switching into a new role could mean a pay cut. Create a budget that paints your full financial picture once in the role, and make sure you can survive on your new salary. Practice living within the new budget for a few months to experience what life would be like.

If you've done the math and can't figure out how to survive on a reduced budget, look outside the box for ways to break even. For instance, you could pick up a side job to help pay down debt. Or you could first build up a nest egg before pursuing your new role. Yes, this could take time. But no one said that your career transition would happen instantaneously.

No matter what, it's up to you to figure out a plan that will let you pursue this new role. Your happiness is worth it.

Put Your Plan in Action

Early in my career, I decided I wanted to move from a management consulting position into a job in media. I had technology and telecommunications experience. At the time, indicators were signaling a convergence of telecommunications, technology, and media into what would soon be known to the world as the iPhone. And I wanted to position myself for this opportunity through gaining a foundation in media. So I set a S.M.A.R.T. goal: I wanted to move, within three months, into a strategic planning role at a local media company, while maintaining or growing my income.

But what did I have to offer a media company? I had skills in technology, telecommunications, consulting, and strategic planning. I also had experience in Six Sigma, which is a strategic approach to process improvement. I reached out to my media colleagues (Network) and asked them to help me identify roles where my skills might be transferable (Assessment). I quickly found an open position at the New York Times Company as a Strategic Planning Manager for Six Sigma. It was a perfect fit.

I used a resume writer who helped me tailor the document for the role at the New York Times Company. In addition, a relative who worked in media helped me put it into the vernacular that would appeal to my eventual hiring manager (Materials). I went to the interview fully prepared, and I impressed them with my knowledge and understanding of the industry, the brand, and their products. I asked the salary range during the interview (Finances), and made sure it was commensurate with what I was currently making.

Sure enough, I got the job that rewarded me with the critical media experience I wanted.

Once you've outlined your career plan, you need to think long and hard about how to execute that plan. It's one thing to know where you're going, but if you don't know how to get there, you'll miss out on the opportunities that hard work has made available to you.

CHAPTER 8

W
A
L
K

Execute the Search

Keep going, no matter what.

—Reginald F. Lewis

Your Interview Execution

My friend Nancy had been at her medical devices company for five years. She was a sales rep but wanted to move into supply chain management. She took courses, prepared, and learned this new field.

When her company had an opening for this position, she applied and landed an interview. She already knew the team, so she figured she'd be a shoo-in. She went into the interview … and completely failed.

Nancy had been so confident of getting the job that she did not prepare. At the interview, the manager grilled her on things she would have known if she had bothered to prepare for the interview. Nancy was devastated.

Luckily for Nancy, she also landed an interview at another company. Determined not to repeat her mistakes, she came to me for help. Together, we applied my process for interview execution and laid out a solid plan. She went to the interview fully prepared, and she got the job.

The interview process is your next step to landing your right-fit job. By following my interview execution process, you will know precisely how to prepare and shine at interviews so that you get job offers. This is the next step in the W part of the L.A.W. method, Walk Toward an Opportunity That Will Make You Happy. This interview process takes you one step closer to a position that aligns with your purpose and creates happiness at work.

Applying Yourself to Getting Your Dream Job

Olympic sprinters spend years preparing for an event that comes down to just a few seconds. The same is true of a job interview. If you've followed the advice outlined in the previous chapters, you're ready. This is what you've been preparing for, so don't shortchange yourself. Kick ass and deliver.

Apply for the job.

Look at company career websites, search on LinkedIn, and especially reach out to your network for job referrals. Forty percent of my jobs have come from personal referrals, and that number tracks with global averages.

To build a foundation of understanding, I look at three different buckets: the industry as a whole, the particular company I'm applying to, and the specific role at that company. For each of those buckets, I have a list of questions I make sure to answer before the interview. The top three questions in each section are listed below.

> Visit my website for more questions:
> ThePursuitOfHappinessAtWork.com.

Industry	Company	Role
• How big is the industry? Is it growing? Declining? Stagnant? Is it crowded? • What is the future outlook for the industry? • Are there any recent changes that have disrupted the industry?	• What does the company do, and what sets it apart from competitors? • How does the company make money? • How old is the company? Does it have staying power?	• How does this role help the company achieve its goals and make money? • What does success look like in this role? • What does career progression look like for this role?

This may seem like a long list. But at the end of the day, you did all the work required to understand yourself—now you need to put the same amount of work into understanding the company, so you can ensure a good match.

Prepare for your interview.

Once you get an interview, don't stop. Keep the momentum going and finish strong.

Build a solid foundation

Having an in-depth understanding of the company's current situation, and how the position you're applying for contributes to that company's future success, will help you differentiate yourself from other candidates. It will also help you see patterns and make connections that others aren't able to make.

Prepare your questions and answers

An interview should be a two-way street. Not only is the company interviewing you, you're also interviewing them. Having prepared questions shows that you're interested in the job and engaged in the process. Questions asked during interviews typically fall into two categories: *Who are you?* and *Why should we hire you?* The better you answer these questions, the greater your chances are for getting the job.

Who are you? questions revolve around your experience and temperament.

- What is your work experience?

- Why do you want to leave your current company?

- What are you passionate about?

- If I talked to your boss, peers, or direct reports, what would they say about you?

- How do you handle stress under pressure?

Why should we hire you? questions focus on your relationship to the role and the company.

- What do you know about our company?

- Why do you want this job?

- What can you offer that no other candidate can?

- Where do you see yourself in five years?

- What are your salary expectations?

Once they finish asking questions, they'll almost always ask whether you have any questions for them. Make sure you have prepared a few good questions that will leave a good impression.

> Visit my website for more questions:
> ThePursuitOfHappinessAtWork.com.

Create your story

At the beginning of an interview, the interviewer may ask you to "Tell me about yourself." Whatever you do, avoid a dry recitation of facts they can get from your resume. Instead, give them a pitch that will leave them asking for more. Here's an example:

"Hi, my name is Brandy. I have a background in public relations, with over five years of experience working for leading companies in both the hospitality and technology industries. I find your company's innovative approach to social media quite extraordinary. In particular, I think that your brand's snarky tone and ability to be in the know with the latest trends

> *is extremely appealing to your target audience,*
> *me being one of them. I was excited to learn*
> *about the opening for a social media manager*
> *in your marketing team, and welcome the*
> *opportunity to put my expertise to work for*
> *your company."*

This pitch was short, yet relevant and informative. An interviewer's natural reaction would be to want to learn more about how Brandy's expertise would help their company.

Practice with mock interviews

You've probably figured out by now that I'm a big planner. Preparation breeds confidence, and confidence always impresses. That's why the next step is a mock interview.

Find someone who can give you a mock interview for the role, and run through it a few times. Give the interviewer prepared questions to include in the mock interview and ask them to add a few questions of their own. Focus not just on what you say, but on how you say it and your body language as you're talking. After the interview, make sure to ask for feedback.

And then do it all again. Practice, practice, and more practice. You have *one shot*. Don't blow it.

Get your head in the game

The night before, make sure you know where you're going and how long it'll take to get there. Print out a few extra copies of your resume and a list of references, just to be prepared.

Once you've done that planning—stop. Get a good night's sleep. Know that you're prepared and you've done everything you can. Feel confident knowing that you're going to go in and do a good job. Just breathe. You're ready to go.

Participate in the Interview.

Arrive fifteen minutes early and check in. Use the restroom, if needed, and then mentally prepare yourself.

Be sure to make a good first impression by greeting your interviewer appropriately with a firm handshake, warm smile, and good eye contact. If someone is designated to come and bring you to the interviewer, treat them with the same courtesy. I can't tell you how many times people have been knocked out of consideration for being rude to administrative assistants or the messenger coming to get them.

If you're given a choice of where to sit, face away from any distractions. You want to give your complete attention to the interviewer. Throughout the interview process, sit up straight, show enthusiasm for the position, and pause for one to two seconds before answering any questions. My wife always tells me that an interview is nothing more than having a conversation. Just let it flow organically, and nine times out of ten you'll do significantly better than if you're sitting there waiting for a firing squad to come at you.

Remember, just as they're trying to get a feel for you, you should also be trying to get a feel for them. The main reason you're putting yourself through all this is to achieve happiness at work. If you don't see yourself being truly happy there, don't get wrapped up in enthusiasm for an offer and take the job anyway. You'll be no better off than you are right now.

Lastly, if the opportunity presents itself at the end of the interview, summarize your skills and abilities concisely and confidently. Reinforce why you think you're the best person for this job. Ask what the next steps are in the hiring process. Make good eye contact, smile, and give a firm handshake. Thank them for their time. Take their contact information, if offered.

Complete your post-interview activities.

The process isn't over when the interview is done. You should *always* send a follow-up email to your interviewers. Thank them for their time and re-emphasize your interest in the position. Include any value add that you might have forgotten. Remember to keep it short, though. You don't want to overwhelm them. If you don't have their email addresses, ask your point of contact for it. If getting the email address is not an option, then ask your point of contact to forward your email to the interviewer. I've definitely knocked people out of consideration for a role because they didn't send thank-you emails.

Finally, take some time to reflect on your recent interview experience. Do you think you did well? Where do you think you can improve? Find time to reflect on everything you know about the industry, the company, the job, the boss, the team, and the role. Will you be happy in this job?

With that, the interview process is over. All that's left is to sit back and see whether you got the job. If not, don't despair. It's time to get back up and try again.

In *The Power of Choice: Embracing Efficacy to Drive Your Career*, Michael Hyter explains the difference between a fixed-capacity mind-set and a capacity-building mind-set.

A person with a fixed-capacity mind-set sees failure as evidence they don't have what it takes to be successful in the new job. This may cause them to reduce their efforts, or even worse, end their pursuit. However, a person with a capacity-building mind-set believes they can learn and become stronger from failure.

When you exercise, you push your muscles to the point of failure when they tear. However, the same way a torn muscle heals and grows stronger, learning from your failures has a similar result. So have a capacity-building mind-set and ask the person who interviewed you or your recruiter how you did. How can you improve next time? What can you do better?

However, if you did get the job, congratulations! You're on your road to happiness. But before you start your new job, let's make sure you know how to negotiate your offer.

CHAPTER 9

W
A
L
K

Mission Accomplished

Don't burn bridges. You'll be surprised how
many times you have to cross the same river.

—H. Jackson Brown Jr.

What Happens After the Offer?

Getting a job offer feels amazing, and it's the goal that
we've been working toward throughout the book.
But once you have an offer in hand, the work isn't
done. You still have to negotiate the details of your
new offer and ensure a smooth transition from your
current role.

I once worked with a colleague named Patricia.
Patricia was a star. She worked with me for seven
years, and every year she was promoted. Patricia's
boss, Barbara, was extremely well respected, not only
in the company but in the industry worldwide.

THE PURSUIT OF HAPPINESS AT WORK

Once Patricia was promoted to senior director, she received invitations to speak at conferences. Soon, recruiters started headhunting her. They knew of Barbara, they had heard about Patricia's amazing work, and they wanted her on their team.

One company offered her a VP position, which came with a juicy executive compensation package. Patricia decided to ask Barbara whether the company would match the offer.

"You've only been senior director for a few months," Barbara said. "I suggest you wait a year, and then we can discuss it."

Unhappy about Barbara's answer, Patricia committed a major no-no and decided to ask Barbara's boss, who went right back to Barbara. Barbara told Patricia that she had eroded her trust by going around her.

Patricia decided to leave and moved to the new company. But two years later, it faced financial challenges, and she was terminated. Patricia applied to many other companies, but her previous boss, Barbara, would not give her a good referral. Eventually, Patricia had to leave the area just to find a job.

Patricia's story shows why it's so important to leave in good stead. Making a smooth transition will help ensure that you can maintain a happy, successful career not just for today but for the long-term. This is the last step of the W in the L.A.W. method, Walk Toward an Opportunity That Will Make You Happy. By keeping your old bridges while building new ones, you strengthen your successful path from your past to your future, ensuring you leave as many opportunities available as possible to fulfill your purpose.

Negotiate Your New Position

Accepting a job is one thing. Negotiating the compensation is another.

There are many things that you can factor into the negotiation:

- Salary. This is pretty straightforward.

- Signing Bonus. Depending on your position and how senior you are, you may get a one-time payment as a signing bonus.

- Vacation. People don't often think about vacation time from a monetary perspective, but the company is actually paying for you to take time for yourself.

- Stock or Shares. Again, whether you have this option will often depend on the role, but it can also depend on the company. Smaller start-ups will often offer stock options to attract strong talent.

- Relocation. If you found a great job with a long commute, you may want to relocate to be closer. Companies will often pay for your move. If the company won't pay for relocation, they may allow you to work from home either part-time or full-time.

- Annual bonus. This is pretty standard.

- Benefits. It's unlikely that you can negotiate how comprehensive your medical or dental benefits are, but you can certainly negotiate whether or not you get them.

These are factors that should be treated as levers that you can pull to achieve your S.M.A.R.T goal.

Don't Burn Your Bridges

Learn from Patricia's mistake. After accepting an offer, you should always leave your job on good terms, regardless of the situation. You could completely hate it and want to burn the place down as they did in the movie *Office Space*. However, you still should leave on good terms.

You do that by giving notice. Two weeks is standard, though it could be longer or shorter depending on the circumstances. Watch how the company has treated other employees and plan accordingly. Some will let you finish out your two weeks, while others will walk you out the door as soon as you give notice.

If you are there for two weeks, create a transition plan that includes detailed documentation of what you do daily. Your goal is to make sure that the person who comes in to fill your role can hit the ground running. They should be able to understand their roles and responsibilities quickly. Ideally, your document will be so clear that your replacement can pick up where you left off and immediately add value. If you do this, both your boss and your replacement will appreciate your efforts.

Another thing you can offer is to help find and train your replacement. Help your boss with the interviews if they'll let you, and try to stagger your replacement's arrival with your leaving so there's a week or two of overlap where you can train them.

When you leave, connect with your co-workers. Send a warm farewell email, even to co-workers you're not particularly fond of. You never know when you might meet them again, especially if you stay in the same industry. Remember your P.I.E.—your performance, your image, and your exposure. You want to make sure that your image—your brand—stays consistent throughout. You never want to leave with someone having a reason to say something bad about you.

If the option is available, request an exit interview. It's a great way to give constructive feedback, and also to show your appreciation for the company. Don't go into the exit interview saying, "I hate this, I hate that," and then walk out with the last word. This isn't your opportunity to get back at the company. It's your way to show your appreciation for what they've done, how they helped you grow.

You can, and should, give constructive feedback on how they could make improvements, but make sure that you manage the person's expectations well. You don't want them to have an image of you as someone who didn't fit the mold of the company. You want to make sure that the person you're interviewing with sees you as a good citizen who simply got a better opportunity.

Before starting a new job, I recommend reading *The First 90 Days* by Michael Watkins. It helps you understand how to hit the ground running and get off on the right foot from day one. Throughout my career, I have read this book before starting a new role, and it has never let me down.

And that's it. You're ready to start a career that fulfills you, that aligns with your purpose, and that brings you success and happiness.

CHAPTER 10

Closing

Don't ever let someone tell you that you can't do something. You got a dream, you gotta protect it. When people can't do something themselves, they are going to tell you that you can't do it. You want something, go get it. Period.

—Chris Gardner, The Pursuit of Happyness

What's next

One of my favorite scenes in *The Pursuit of Happyness* is when Chris lands an interview for his dream job. As you know, the movie is based on the real-life experiences of Chris Gardner, as portrayed by Will Smith. By the time of the interview, Chris had been homeless for some time and was raising his young son on the streets, all while training for his ideal job as an investment broker.

In this scene, Chris, arriving straight from jail, wears an undershirt and pants covered with paint stains.

THE PURSUIT OF HAPPINESS AT WORK

But during the interview, Chris shares what he can bring to the firm, his passion for the work, and how it's not just a job, but a chance at a career that uses his talents for the betterment of himself and the company. The company leaders offer him the internship.

In real life, Chris Gardner eventually started his own successful investment firm and wrote the bestselling memoir of his journey.

At the beginning of this journey, I asked you, "Where is your happiness?" I hope you see how you can achieve happiness in both your work and life. That you can land a job that draws on your unique strengths, with a boss who supports your growth, and a healthy work environment that sustains you.

By following the steps laid out in this book, you will be able to define happiness at work, make adjustments in the job you have, or plan a way to move on. You will be able to use the L.A.W. method to succeed and achieve your purpose by "**Learning** Your Definition of Happiness at Work," "**Assessing** Whether You Are Happy in Your Role," and "**Walking** Toward an Opportunity That Will Make You Happy."

You have the tools to achieve happiness, and you know how to apply your efforts to achieve results. You're ready to align with your purpose, with your happiness. But as you set out, remember that your career isn't a sprint. It's a marathon.

Things change. Your company may face financial challenges. Your boss may leave and be replaced by someone whose style is a bad fit. The company could pivot, and your projects could change. You could outgrow your position, or learn new things about yourself and discover a new direction you want to tap into.

With those changes, feel free to reach out and continue the conversation. Keep asking questions, and keep moving toward your ideal. You can find me on ThePursuitOfHappinessAtWork.com, Twitter, LinkedIn, and various social media channels. I'm also available for public speaking engagements and book signings. I want to talk to you about how to live your purpose, and help you find personal ways to achieve happiness at work. Everyone is different, and it's never the wrong time to start on the path.

My own pursuit of happiness at work has brought immense satisfaction. Using the guide I've shared with you, I now truly appreciate the role I'm in, the people I work with, the environment I have, and the type of work I'm doing. And having experienced that, I diligently protect it. I constantly do the work to make sure I'm managing my perspective. I do everything I can to foster a caring environment, especially in my relationships with my boss and my peers. I consistently find ways to use my natural abilities to help me be successful. And as crazy as this road has been, I can say that I am extremely happy.

In *Don't Waste Your Talent,* Bob McDonald and Don Hutcheson talk about this phenomenon of True Self vs. System Self. Within yourself, you have your True Self and what we call a System Self. The System Self is the version of yourself you have to put on around systems, such as work. Your True Self is your heart. Your essence. Who you were when you were three years old.

Without introspection, those two selves can get out of alignment. Moving these selves back toward each other can cause an earthquake. It's a huge disruption. And while that disruption can have negative effects, the alignment itself is a good thing, for it creates balance.

The steps in this book will help you get back to alignment. Embrace the earthquake. Let it move you, because when you move into alignment, everything will be different. You'll live your purpose and find happiness at work.

The Road Onward

In my dedication, I shared a quote by Mark Twain: "The two most important days in your life are the day you are born and the day you find out why." I know my why.

My purpose is bringing people together and helping them to achieve happiness in their lives and their careers. That's why I wrote this book, and it's why I continue to teach the principles of the pursuit for happiness at work. I want to help you find your purpose and your strength, so that you can find your own personal brand of success. Everyone deserves that happiness. Thank you, readers, for taking this quick but meaningful journey with me.

Your pursuit of happiness at work starts now.

ABOUT THE AUTHOR

James Nixon is an author, corporate strategist, technology innovation executive, and career consultant. He teaches individuals and leaders how to improve their overall performance and career success by making happiness at work a priority.

In *The Pursuit of Happiness at Work,* James draws from his extensive experience in digital strategy and innovation at Hilton, CNN, Microsoft, Deloitte, Marriott, The New York Times, and others to offer a fresh perspective on how to align personal goals with professional pursuits to create meaningful change in your life.

Nixon holds an MBA from the Johnson Graduate School of Management at Cornell University and a BS in Computer Engineering from Lehigh University.

Printed in Great Britain
by Amazon